Second Edition

Gratitude
+Grace

Growth
A 31–Day Devotional

Second Edition

Gratitude +Grace

Growth

A 31–Day Devotional

Lisa Cassman

Halo
PUBLISHING
INTERNATIONAL

Halo Publishing International
7550 WIH-10 #800, PMB 2069,
San Antonio, TX 78229

Second Edition, May 2024
ISBN: 978-1-63765-609-9
Library of Congress Control Number: 2024909195

Halo Publishing International is a self-publishing company that publishes adult fiction and non-fiction, children's literature, self-help, spiritual, and faith-based books. We continually strive to help authors reach their publishing goals and provide many different services that help them do so. We do not publish books that are deemed to be politically, religiously, or socially disrespectful, or books that are sexually provocative, including erotica. Halo reserves the right to refuse publication of any manuscript if it is deemed not to be in line with our principles. Do you have a book idea you would like us to consider publishing? Please visit www.halopublishing.com for more information.

My life is where it's at because of God and the people He has put in my life.

Steve, as you support and encourage me in all I do and all I have accomplished.

Also, Allison, Angela, and Audrey, you have been such blessings to me. Thank you for your friendship.

CONTENTS

INTRODUCTION

As you journey through this devotional, you'll find a prayer guide in each day's write up. But don't let your prayers end there! Let the daily prayer guide be only the beginning. Here are four ways to pray to God which you can be mindful of:

1. Praise and be thankful

2. In silence—wait upon the Lord

3. Confess and pray for your needs

4. Intercession—pray for others

Section One

Gratitude

DAY 1

GRATITUDE

Rejoice always, pray continually, give
thanks in all circumstances; for this is God's
will for you in Christ Jesus.

1 Thessalonians 5:16–18

Our lives can be so busy and feel so empty, but by trusting God, you can know that life can feel fulfilled, and you can feel loved.

Think of something that you haven't been able to let go of but know that you need to. Today, tell God you are thankful for His help in working through it. Take it a step further and write it down. Even if at this moment you aren't able to let the emptiness go, God will help you. He wants you to give thanks for all things, even the little things that you may feel you have no control over. We all get busy and forget to take the time to focus on what He has done for us or is doing for us even now. Let's not overlook it today.

Prayer

God, thank you for all you have done for me and all you are going to do to help me move forward. Show me what I need to let go of and help me give thanks knowing that you will heal me.

DAY 2

GRATITUDE

Do not be anxious about anything, but in
every situation, by prayer and petition, with
thanksgiving, present your requests to God.
And the peace of God, which transcends all
understanding, will guard your hearts and
your minds in Christ Jesus.

Philippians 4:6–7

Anxiety plays a part when we are not comfortable in what is going on in our lives, when we have no control over a situation, and when we don't know what is going to happen. It could be something such as the illness of a loved one, a death, the loss of a job, or even our children or other family members distancing themselves and not talking to us.

God will guard your heart against the negative thoughts; you just need to trust Him.

Write down some things that are causing you to be anxious. What can you do differently to help yourself get past the thoughts?

Prayer

God, help me to understand what is happening even if I don't know why it is happening. Help me to hand it to you and not try to carry it on my own.

DAY 3

GRATITUDE

**But thanks be to God! He gives us victory
through our Lord Jesus Christ.**

1 Corinthians 15:57

In the midst of it all, God knows how things will turn out. He knows our hearts and the outcome of every situation. It will be a victory! It may not be what we wanted it to be or expected, but it is His will and His way.

What are some things that you are asking God for? You may not see the end result as a victory, but God knows what He's doing, and you will have peace as you trust Him.

As you ponder this, write five victories that God has given to you in the past. How have they changed your life?

Prayer

God, thank you for always being faithful, even if I don't feel it in my heart. Thank you for giving me the answers that are always perfect, even if I don't see it at the time. You know how to turn tragedy into triumph.

Day 4

Gratitude

We ought always to thank God for you, brothers and sisters, and rightly so, because your faith is growing more and more, and the love all of you have for one another is increasing.

2 Thessalonians 1:3

You may not see growth in your fellow brothers and sisters, but that is not for you to judge. Only God knows each of our hearts, and He knows where we all are with Him.

ENcourage each other—don't DIScourage, as so many are in the habit of doing. Can you think of a time when you felt good about something you were doing, and someone was trying to hold you back? What did you do, and how did you react?

Today, write down the names of five people that you can encourage. Then take the time to either call, write, or go see those people to let them know you appreciate them.

Prayer

God, help me to see the best in others and not to be judgmental. Help me to understand and encourage anyone who may be hurting. Help me to recognize where they may be coming from and what they have been through, even if I don't know all the details. Take all of me, Lord, and allow me to see others through your eyes.

DAY 5

GRATITUDE

**Give thanks to the Lord, for he is good;
his love endures forever.**

1 Chronicles 16:34

Do you pray only when you need something from God, or do you thank and praise Him during the things He has done for you also, knowing and trusting that they are from God?

What are you thankful for today? Can you give thanks to the Lord just because He is who He is, and you know that He is good? Give thanks to God because He is who He says He is, and He will love you forever. What are some things He has done for you? Before you pray for needs, thank Him for what He has done.

Prayer

God, please help me to be thankful for all you have done, even when I don't always feel like being thankful. Thank you for loving me and giving me the gift of salvation so I can live a life that glorifies you. Help me become a person who can be an example to others. Thank you for a love that will never fail or end.

DAY 6

GRATITUDE

Every good gift and every perfect gift is
from above, coming down from the Father
of lights with whom there is no variation or
shadow due to change.

James 1:7

We are not talking about material gifts; we are talking about the gifts from above. What are some of the gifts from God that you are thankful for? God has given us so many things: the gift of salvation, speaking to him, and teaching, plus many more.

Understanding what God has for you is a great gift. He doesn't harm you; He just wants you to know how much He loves you! His greatest gift to us is salvation!

Prayer

God, thank you for your many gifts that you have given to me, but also to others so we may work together for your good. Help me to do my best to bring out the best in others. Give me the knowledge that I need, in tune with your Spirit, to do the work your love has assigned for me. And please give me the strength to do it, too.

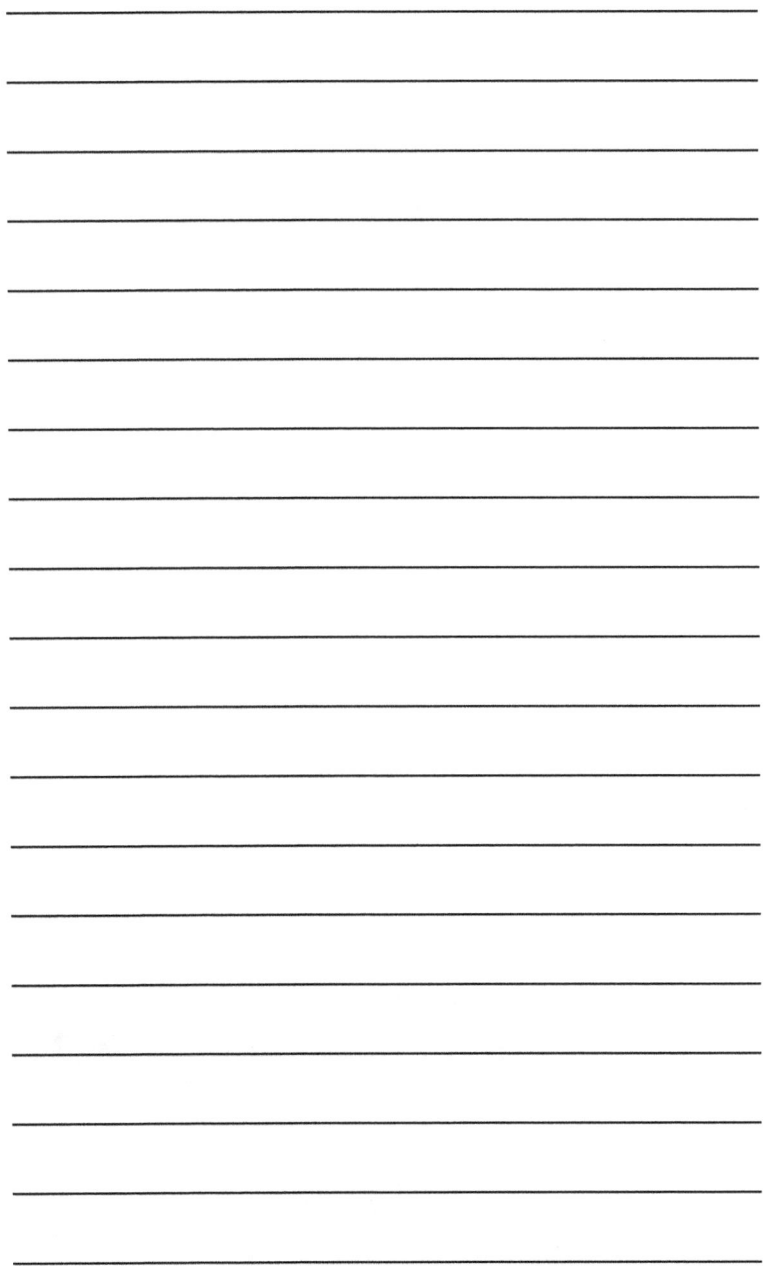

DAY 7

GRATITUDE

**I will give thanks to you, Lord, with all my
heart; I will tell of all your wonderful deeds.**

Psalm 9:1

What are the wonderful things God has done for you? Who will you tell? Are you willing to share with the world the love that He gave us? John 3:16 says it all: He gave his one and only Son so we can have eternal life.

Some days you may not feel like He has done anything for you and that He doesn't care, but He does care.

We tend to look at the things He does not do for us. Imagine your children are young, and you do so many great things for their good, but they only see the times when you don't give them what they want. You, being the parent, knew that thing wasn't something they actually needed at the time. That is how our God is; He does what is best for us and answers our prayers accordingly, but He also gives us so much, and we don't always see the answers the way we expected them to be. We that feel in order for Him to be good, it means He should always give us what we want.

Are you sharing the goodness of God? Or are you complaining about what He hasn't done for you?

Prayer

God, thank you for your wonderful deeds you have done for me. Help me to understand that the way you answer is what is best for me. You have done so much for me, but the best gift you have given is the free gift of salvation, to have you live in my heart and life. Help me to share with the world what you have done for me. Thank you, God, for all your wonderful deeds, but especially for the greatest of all: sending your Son to die on the cross to give me eternal life and the freedom to worship you and live a life of love and forgiveness in my heart. Thank you for giving us love everlasting.

_____

_____

_____

_____

_____

_____

_____

_____

_____

_____

_____

_____

DAY 8

GRATITUDE

And whatever you do, whether in word or deed, do it all in the name of the Lord Jesus, giving thanks to God the Father through Him.

Colossians 3:17

It is always great to do things for others, but don't do it to the extent that you hurt yourself. When you overextend yourself, you will start to feel that others are using you. So while it is great to help others, do it in the name of the Lord. Pray so you have peace about it and know that it is what God wants for you to do. Sometimes we have a tendency to keep doing things for others to the point that we aren't taking care of ourselves. Keep a balance in your life.

Who can you do some good deeds for? No matter how big or small, do them in the Lord's name. Are you taking care of yourself and doing what is good for your health and body? What can you do for yourself?

Prayer

God, please help me to take care of myself so I can help others and feel healthy at the same time. Give me strength to walk in your ways and breathe when I need to. Help me find the balance between taking care of myself and doing things for others, so I can do it all for your glory.

DAY 9

GRATITUDE

Let the peace of Christ rule in your hearts,
since as members of one body you were
called to peace. And be thankful.

Colossians 3:15

You may have had someone hurt you so badly that you don't feel peace in your mind and heart anymore. Has someone in the church hurt you? It can be such a big betrayal knowing that the ones you trusted the most have hurt you in what had felt like a safe space.

Write down who has hurt you and what you can do to help yourself feel better. God wants us to forgive; are you ready for that? You can have the peace that he has offered us. You may not be able to work with them at this time, but you can forgive. God wants us to be thankful for what we have learned. God wants you to be able to trust again. To have that security in your life is so important.

Prayer

God, help me to give all my hurts to you. I want the peace that you have offered me and the love that comes with it. I am going to trust that you will help all those involved in this hurt to come to that peace in their hearts. Thank you for the body of Christ that works together. I want to forgive those who have hurt me, but I also want to forgive myself.

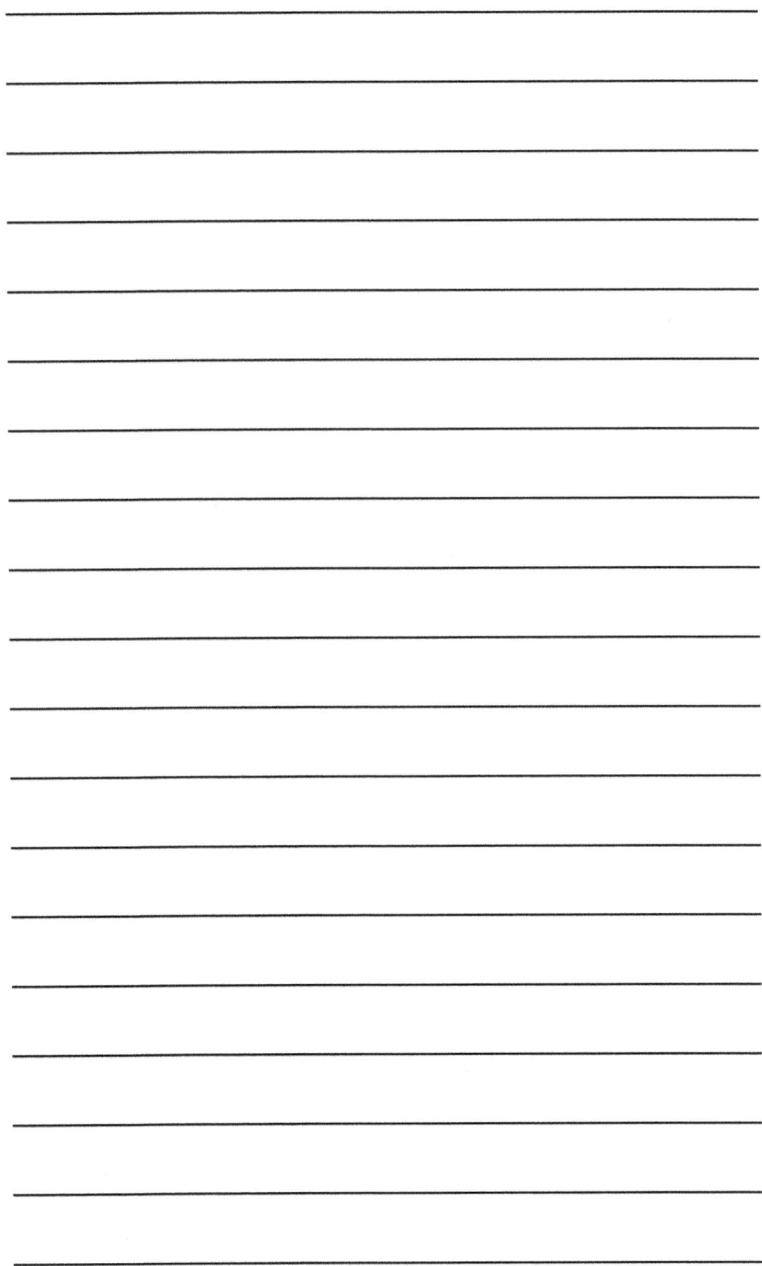

DAY 10

GRATITUDE

**Devote yourselves to prayer,
being watchful and thankful.**

Colossians 4:2

PRAY! PRAY! PRAY! Do you spend time in prayer? Matthew 21:22 says, "Whatever you ask in prayer, believing you shall receive." Are you praying in desperation or when you are thankful? You should be doing both, as God wants you to devote yourself in prayer all the time, not just when you need something.

Are you doing great today or having a bad day? Write down some prayers of things to be thankful for and some prayers of things that need some healing.

You can overcome all things through Christ. Be watchful and thank Him for what He has done and is about to do.

Prayer

God, I want to thank you for the life you have given me—not just the great things that have happened, but the things I know you are going to do for me. I may have had some setbacks, but that's okay. You will walk me through them and get me to the sense of love and trust that I need with you.

DAY 11

GRATITUDE

You will be enriched in every way so that
you can be generous on every occasion, and
through us your generosity will result in
thanksgiving to God.

2 Corinthians 9:11

We like to think that when we have very little to give, we don't need to. I believe in tithing. Even if it's your last dollar, God will provide for you. In Mark 12:41–44, the poor widow gave two small copper coins, but because it was all she had, she gave more than the rich.

I knew I didn't have a lot of money, but God told me to give it to someone in need. When I obeyed, I was blessed back by God and taken care of.

Be thankful for what God has given you. He wants you to know that it is from Him. And just as He provided you with that, He will continue to provide.

Give your time for God, also. You will be blessed by knowing you have done what God has asked you to do. Don't do it for selfish reasons; do it for God. What can you do for God?

Prayer

God, help me to see where I can help others and to trust in you to tithe. Show me where you want me to give back to you. Help me to trust you in the area of giving and not just think of myself.

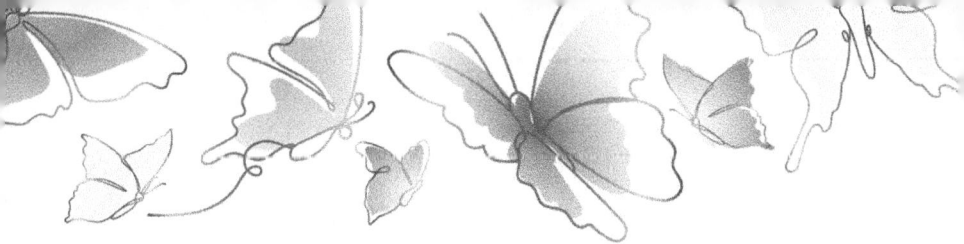

DAY 12

GRATITUDE

Let the message of Christ dwell among
you richly as you teach and admonish one
another with all wisdom through psalms,
hymns, and songs from the Spirit, singing
to God with gratitude in your hearts.

Colossians 3:16

Start your day by praying and putting on worship music. Take time to sing your heart out to God.

What are some of your favorite songs for telling God how you feel? Your life isn't just about you; you can open it to God and share your life with Him. He wants you to trust Him and feel the anointing of His Spirit on you.

Your heart will feel lighter and freer while you enter into His presence. If you don't think you have a voice that can sing, God loves to hear it coming from your heart. I encourage you to put on worship music while saying this prayer and really open your heart to God.

Prayer

God, I am going to allow my heart to really open to you and have you come in so I can feel your anointing. Help me to feel your presence and the love you have for me. I give you my all today. Forgive me and cleanse my heart!

Day 13

Gratitude

And he took bread, gave thanks and broke it, and gave it to them, saying, "This is my body given for you; do this in remembrance of me."

Luke 22:19

And when he had taken a cup and given thanks, he gave it to them saying, "Drink from it, all of you."

Matthew 26:27

How are you feeling? Is your heart right with God? Write down some things you're carrying that you want to give to God.

Jesus died on the cross so we can have life everlasting. John 3:16 says, "For God so loved the world He gave his one and only son that whoever believes in Him shall not perish but have eternal life."

He didn't die for just one person; He died so we can all have that eternal life. I encourage you to really look at your heart today. Can you say that you are committed to God?

Take something to represent Jesus's body and blood, and do your own private Communion table with him. I encourage you to take this for what it symbolizes.

Prayer

God, I search my heart to make sure it is pure and clean for you. Forgive me, as I know I need to open up my heart and all my life to you.

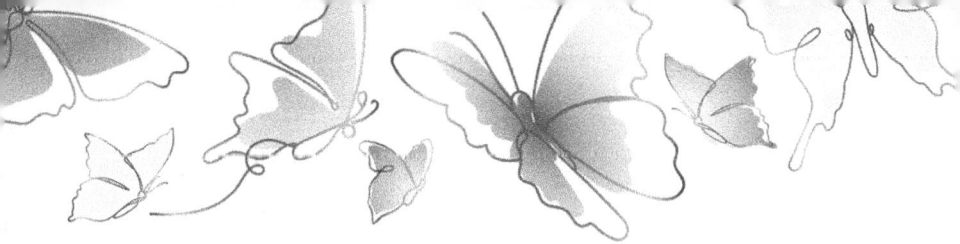

DAY 14

GRATITUDE

This is the day the Lord has made,
let us rejoice and be glad in it.

Psalm 118:24

Wake up and say this scripture every morning: "This is the day the Lord has made, let us rejoice and be glad in it!"

He made each day. We all have setbacks, but God is there with you. He doesn't walk away from you. Make the best of what you have and who you are. Is your life perfect? No! Is every situation or person perfect? No! But God is still in control, and He loves you so much.

What are some things you can rejoice about? What are you thankful for?

Prayer

God, help me to see the good in each day. Help me to trust that you have everything in control in your timing. I want to see the best in everyone and all situations.

Day 15

Gratitude

Enter his gates with thanksgiving,
and his courts with praise! Give thanks
to him; bless his name!

Psalm 100:4

Open your heart to praise God not just today, but every day. Find that song that can lift your spirits and give God the glory due to Him while also giving you the encouragement you need for the day. Encourage yourself to spend time in song with God, and open your heart to what He has for you. Don't be in a hurry, really open your heart and wait for Him to fill it.

What are some songs that can help you connect with an awareness of His presence today?

Prayer

God, I enter into your presence today. You are high and lifted up! You are the light of the world.

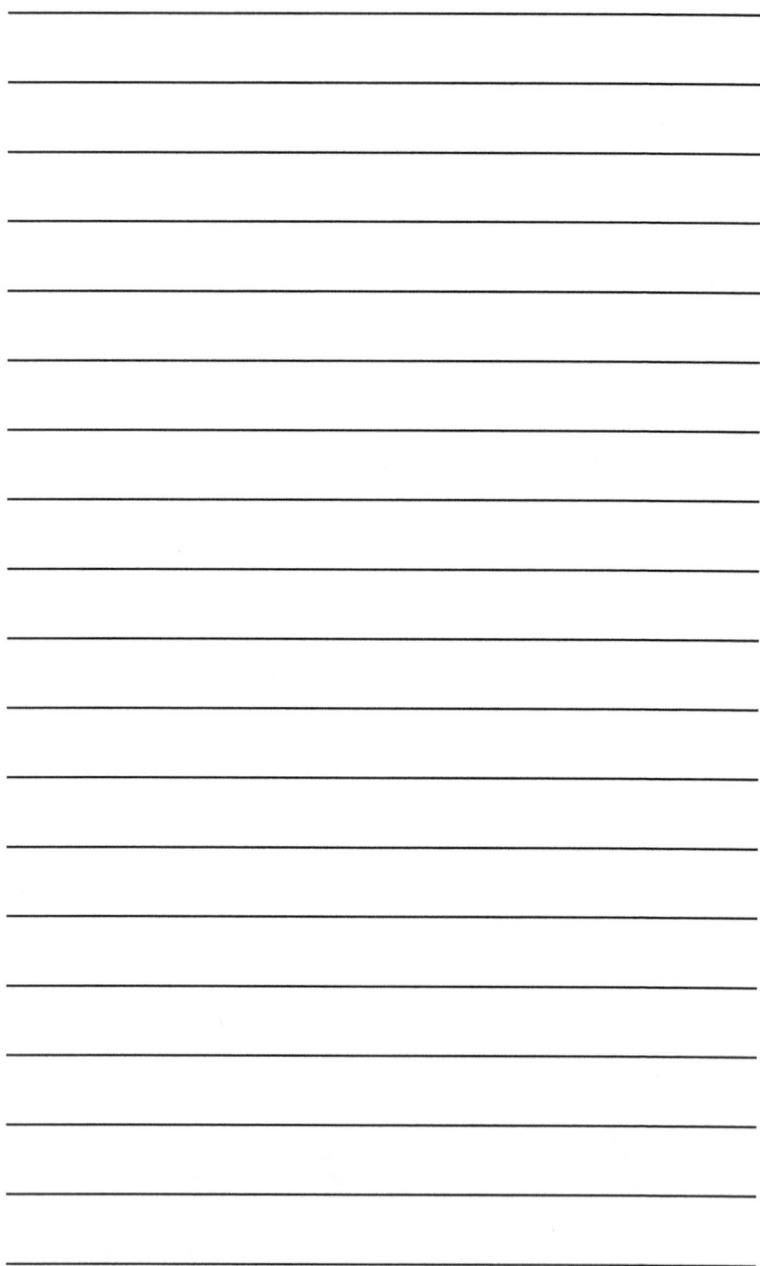

GRATITUDE CHECK-IN

We've just spent 15 days looking at gratitude. Spend some time today checking in on where your heart is when it comes to the amount of gratitude you practice in your life. Every so often, come back here and use these questions to check in again—you can write future answers in a journal or on another piece of paper if you've already written in the space here. You might start to see your life transformed by the spirit of gratitude that you cultivate!

How is your day going? What has happened to have you feeling this way?

_____

_____

_____

_____

_____

_____

There will have been positive moments you may not have taken the time to notice. Think back and write down something positive that has happened today:

_____

_____

_____

_____

_____

_____

Something you did for which you can pat yourself on the back:

_____

_____

_____

_____

_____

_____

Something you did that took courage:

_____

_____

_____

_____

_____

_____

_____

Today, I can forgive myself for...

_____

_____

_____

_____

_____

_____

The most wonderful thing about being alive is...

_____

_____

_____

_____

_____

_____

Find an opportunity this week to commit an act of kindness.

Being kind to others will help you feel better about yourself. This week's acts of kindness could be as simple as complimenting someone whom you feel needs a boost in their confidence, a kind note, a small gift, or a thoughtful act of service. You can make notes here:

_____

_____

_____

_____

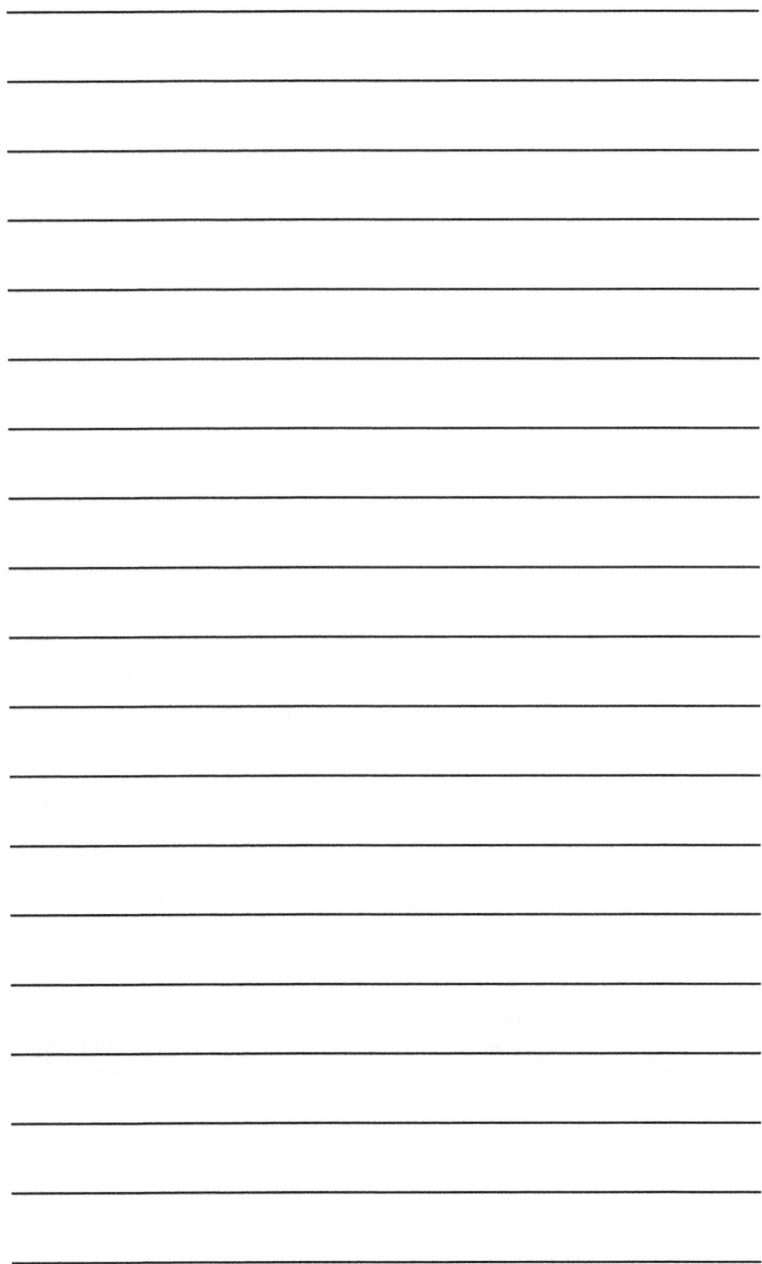

SECTION TWO

GRACE

Consider making an act of kindness an
intentional weekly practice going forward!

Day 16

Grace

But He said to me, "My grace is sufficient for you, for my power is made perfect in weakness." Therefore I will boast all the more gladly of my weaknesses, so that the power of Christ may rest upon me.

2 Corinthians 12:9

We know that God's grace is enough for us, but we sometimes don't know how to put it into practice.

Take a moment and write down 10 areas in which you feel you have a weakness toward sin. Ask God to help you through so that you can feel His life-changing grace in those areas. As you write, look up and listen to the song "His Grace is Sufficient for Me." Really take the words in and accept his grace.

Prayer

God, I give you all my weaknesses so that I can feel your strength and endurance in my life. I know that your grace is sufficient for me. Help me have the courage to boast about your works and to let others know what you have done for me.

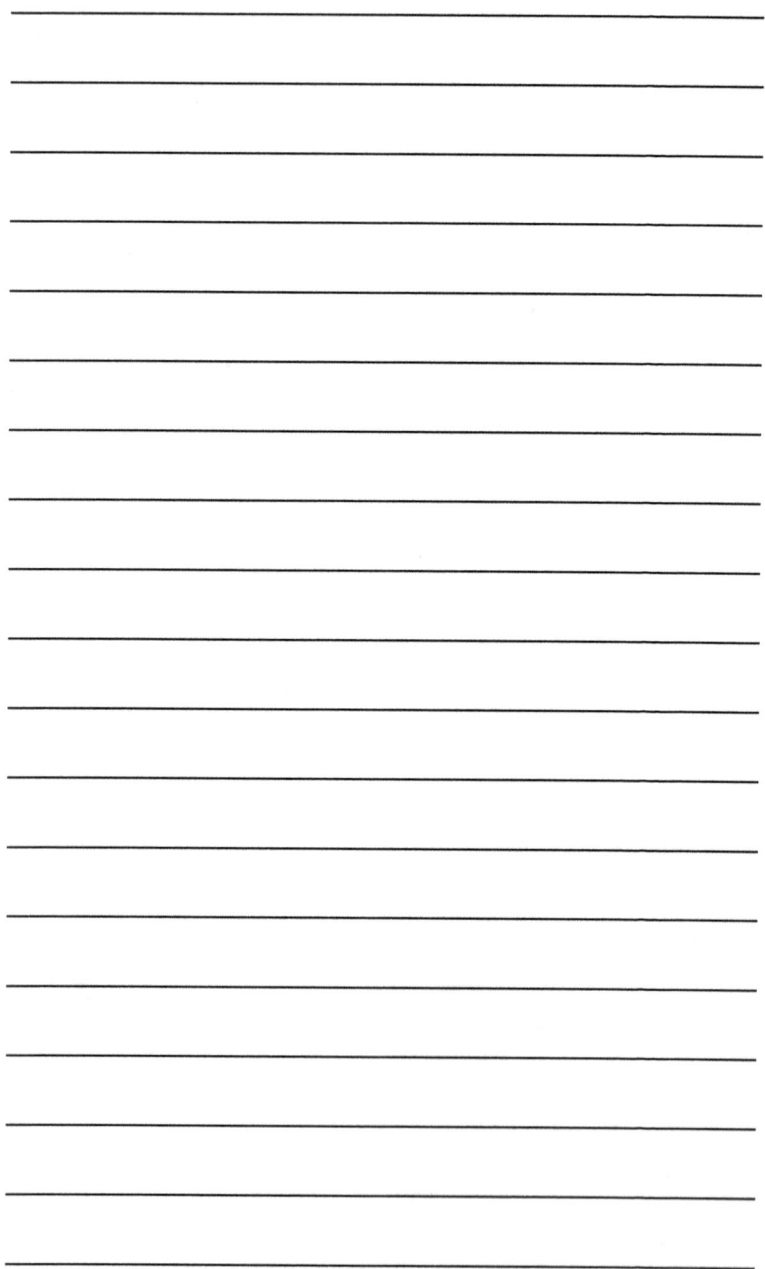

DAY 17

GRACE

**For sin will have no dominion over you,
since you are not under law but under grace.**

Romans 6:14

God has given us the power to ask for forgiveness. Once we have confessed our sin and asked for forgiveness, we will have that sin behind us and won't have to dwell on it or let it influence our future.

Allow God to take it and keep it behind you so you won't have to carry it anymore. When you ask Him for forgiveness, He will forgive you, and you have grace and life everlasting.

What are some things you have done that you have asked forgiveness for but feel you haven't been forgiven for? Write it on a sheet of paper, and then take it and tell God that you don't want to carry it…rip it up, throw it away, and let it go.

Prayer

God, thank you for the love you have for me. Thank you for taking the sin so I don't have to carry it with me and think about it day and night. Thank you for your forgiveness.

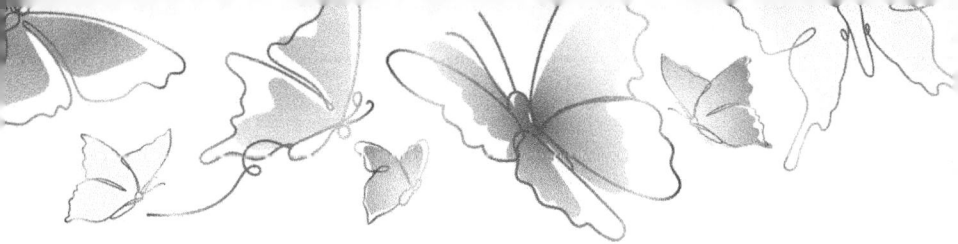

DAY 18

GRACE

But if it is by grace, it is no longer on the basis of works; otherwise grace would no longer be grace.

Romans 11:6

Your works will not get you salvation; your life and how you live will. When you know you are saved by God's son shedding his blood, you will feel the grace in your heart and your life. Keep doing His work, but know it is what is in your heart that gives you eternal life.

What are some ways you can do God's work behind the scenes instead of out where everyone knows what you're doing?

Prayer

God, help me to live my life as an example of how you want us to live. Allow my heart to be open to live the life that keeps me from straying away from your will, knowing that the works I do will not get me to heaven, but what I have in my heart will. Help me to understand the difference and keep doing your work as you have given me the ability and the grace to do.

DAY 19

GRACE

But he gives more grace. Therefore it says,
"God opposes the proud, but gives grace
to the humble."

James 4:6

Many of us like to brag about what we do for the Lord, but His word clearly states that we should be humble. Open your mind to see what God can do when you stay behind the scenes.

Can you think of something you have done that you have bragged about, but it didn't withstand what you expected? What can you do for God without letting everyone know what you're doing to help transform people's lives with Jesus?

Living as an example of someone devoted to Christ is the best thing to do. Live it to your fullest potential, and don't brag about what you have done. One thing to share openly, though, is testimonies of how we've been changed by Christ from doing things we shouldn't have done and how His grace transformed our lives.

Think about some things that you've learned from in your own testimony which you can use to help others with. How and why have you changed the way you have done things?

Prayer

God, humble me with your presence and help me to grow into the example for others that you'd like me to be. Help me to keep your light shining bright in me and not shout out what I am doing for you, but instead only shout about what you have done for me. Thank you for your light in this world which can be so dark.

_____

_____

_____

_____

_____

_____

_____

_____

_____

_____

_____

_____

_____

_____

_____

_____

DAY 20

GRACE

For by grace you have been saved through
faith. And this is not your own doing;
it is the gift of God.

Ephesians 2:8

While you were still a sinner, when you weren't living for the Lord, did you believe that there was one true God who saved us, or did you feel that God wasn't real? How strongly do you believe that God is here to save you, so that your salvation is by grace and not by your own doing? Describe how you felt after you received salvation through your faith.

Prayer

God, I ask you to help me with faith, enough to know that only you can save me. I ask you to help me grow each day in knowing that salvation is a gift from you. Teach me to be accountable to who you are and trust you enough to know that I am loved.

DAY 21

GRACE

**As each has received a gift, use it
to serve one another, as good stewards
of God's varied grace.**

1 Peter 4:10

God has asked that we utilize the gifts he has given us. Search your heart and ask God what your giftings are. Sometimes God will tell us or show us what He has given us, but we don't see it his way. We want to do things our way. But if we trust God and obey, we will be blessed beyond what we can ever imagine.

He will strengthen you and show you how what you do for Him will bless someone else who you may not even know you're blessing. Being a blessing keeps you grounded—it ends up blessing you more than the blessing you think you're giving!

What are your gifts, and what are some ways you can use them to help others?

Prayer

God, I ask you for guidance with the gifts you have given me. Help me to understand your will for me to use them to help others so they may see the truth of your love through me. Take my heart, Lord, and let my life be used for your glory.

Day 22

Grace

And after you have suffered a little while, the God of all grace, who has called you to his eternal glory in Christ, will himself restore, confirm, strengthen, and establish you.

1 Peter 5:10

Likewise, you who are younger, be subject to the elders. Clothe yourselves, all of you, with humility toward one another, for "God opposes the proud but gives grace to the humble."

1 Peter 5:5

Have you had to go through trials, and did you feel like you were suffering? Even if it felt like a big deal at the time, you soon understood that God has everything under control, even if you don't understand why it may have happened.

This verse is showing us that when we suffer, God will strengthen and restore us; we just need a little faith. Matthew 17:20 tells us we only need faith the size of a mustard seed. Do you have that faith? What is something that you have had to suffer through, only to realize that God is in control when he restored you?

Are you going through something now that you need to trust that God will take you through? Can you think of some mature believers in your life who you might ask to pray for you and with you?

Prayer

God, you have promised to restore me and give me grace. I ask you to give me the strength to trust you as I go through the trying times I'm in. Life may not be good to me, but I know that you are. Humble my spirit to reach out to those who can pray with me in this season of struggle.

DAY 23

GRACE

But grow in the grace and knowledge
of our Lord and Savior Jesus Christ.
To Him be the glory both now
and to the day of eternity. Amen.

2 Peter 3:18

Keep reading God's Word. He has so much to offer and so much more to give than we know or understand. I challenge you to take your Bible each day and read some scripture. Pray and ask God what He wants you to know and get from it.

Decide now what scripture you are going to read the next five days. Take it a step further and find a book to read that someone has written on the very topic you have been studying. Maybe write down what the scripture spoke to you and tuck it there in your bible to find again another day.

Prayer

God, I ask you for your guidance and understanding of your word. Show me what you are saying to me. Help me to open my heart to your works so that I may understand your grace more each day. Let me be an example to others who have been searching for your grace.

DAY 24

GRACE

The Lord is not slow to fulfill his promise as
some count slowness, but is patient toward
you, not wishing that any should perish, but
that all should reach repentance.

2 Peter 3:9

God has so much patience for us. We may feel like He doesn't answer our prayers, but He knows exactly what, how, and when He wants something for us. How patient are you? Imagine your children wanting something that you know you just don't want them to have. Like God, parents don't have to give their children everything they ask for. Be patient to wait for what He does want you to have.

What is something you asked for but didn't receive, and instead He gave you something far better than you could have ever imagined?

Take a moment to think about something that you felt hurt about when you asked God for it and didn't receive it. Remember that He wants you to repent and be born again. He loves you so much. He longs for you to open your heart to Him.

Prayer

God, I understand that life can be unfair. Please help me to understand that what you have for me isn't always going to be what I want. Help me to understand that I need to trust you, even if my mind is full of questions. Your ways are higher than I can perceive of. I repent of my sins and come to you for guidance with an open heart.

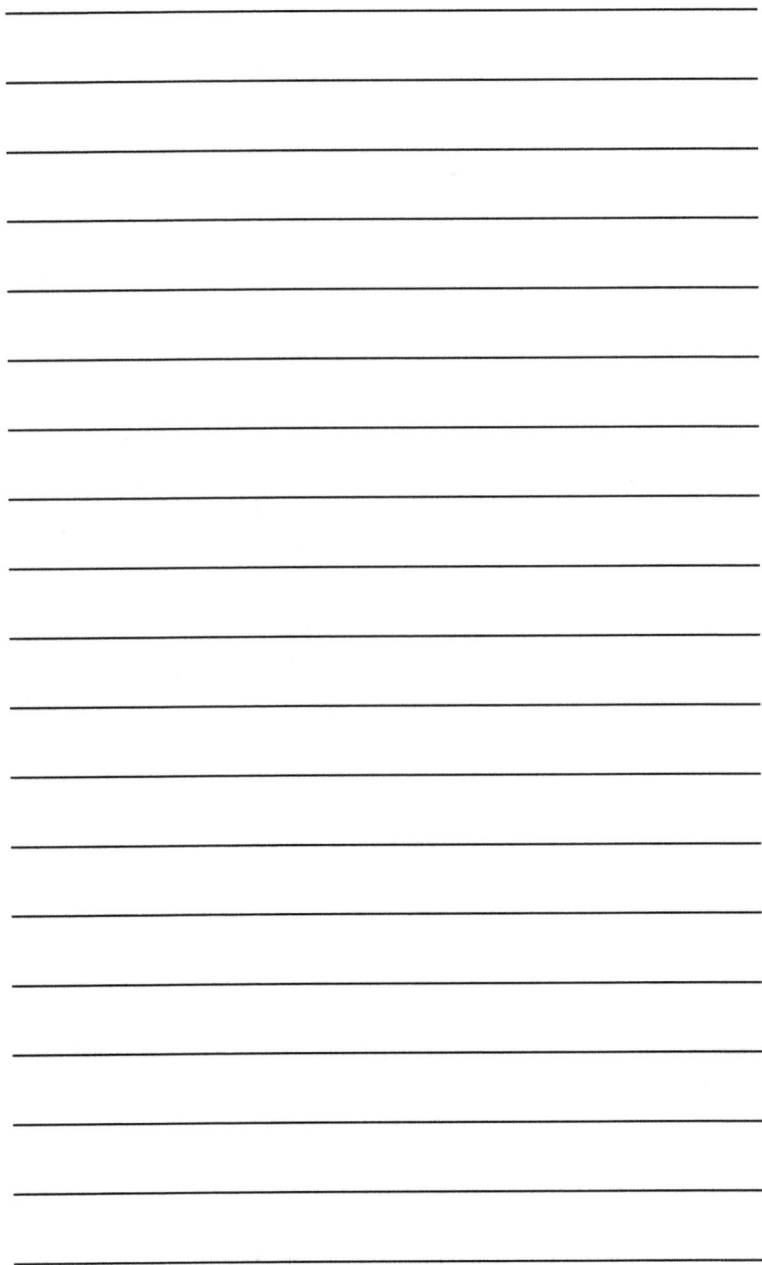

DAY 25

GRACE

Who saved us and called us to a holy calling,
not because of our works but because of his
own purpose and grace, which he gave us in
Christ Jesus before the ages began.

2 Timothy 1:9

You then, my child, be strengthened by the
grace that is in Christ Jesus.

2 Timothy 2:1

But we believe that we will be saved through
the grace of the Lord Jesus, just as they will.

Acts 15:11

We will not get to heaven by our works, but by His grace and love that He has shown to those who have repented and become a new person. Take time to listen to what He has given us, and know in our hearts that someday we will see Him in heaven. Let your light shine for Him, and walk in His ways. Take a moment to reflect on your life. Have you thought that the work you do will get you saved or earn God's grace?

He still wants you to do his work; it just won't get you to heaven.

Prayer

God, please help me to see that the love you have for me is far greater than the works I may have done or am doing. Help me to see that I need your grace and forgiveness; doing works in your name won't cut it. Show me what you want me to do, and show me how to live the life you want me to. Give me strength to live the life you want me to.

DAY 26

GRACE

But they who wait for the Lord shall renew their strength; they shall mount up with wings like eagles; they shall run and not be weary; they shall walk and not faint.

Isaiah 40:31

For God so loved the world, that He gave his only Son, that whoever believes in him should not perish but have eternal life.

John 3:16

The Lord makes his face to shine upon you and be gracious to you.

Numbers 6:25

And we are justified by his grace as a gift, through the redemption that is in Christ Jesus.

Romans 3:24

Are you feeling weak today? How about yesterday? When was the last time you had strength to just move ahead and go about the day as God intended? Have you lost sight of what the prize is and let weakness take over?

Today's scripture tells us that we shall mount up on wings like eagles. An eagle has a wide wingspan and has a lot of strength to do what it needs to get done. Write down some things that have gotten you down and make you feel like the world is treating you unfairly and you have no strength to go on.

Write down what you feel that God can do for you in this moment to get your strength back. Do you trust Him enough to keep going with Him, knowing that He is doing what is best for you?

Prayer

God, please help me to open my eyes to see that strength comes from you, and that I don't need to feel down and lonely because you are my friend. You have given your son, Jesus, to die for me. Thank you for the life I can lead with you always by my side.

DAY 27

GRACE

**But God shows his love for us in that while
we were still sinners, Christ died for us.**

Romans 5:8

**For the grace of God has appeared, bringing
salvation for all people.**

Titus 2:11

Have you received the gift of salvation? This is a gift that cannot be replaced with any earthly physical gifts.

Take a moment to really think about what God has done for you, and write down what He has done for you. Life can throw us in so many different directions, but we know that no matter what happens, God has given us His Son, and that it will be okay.

Prayer

God, I ask you into my life. Please take away my sins. Help me live my life for you, and show me how to be an example to others who I come into contact with.

DAY 28

GRACE

Waiting for our blessed hope,
the appearance of the glory of our
great God and Savior Jesus Christ.

Titus 2:13

While going through trials and not knowing what tomorrow will bring, are you patient as you wait for answers? Or do you try to take things into your own hands? We can put our trust in Jesus and know there is hope in Him.

What are some things that have happened to you that left you close to losing hope? What did you do to turn that into believing God, content in what He has for you and knowing there is hope? What did God do to open your heart?

Prayer

Thank you, God, for the hope you have given us in knowing that you are coming back for us someday. I want to be ready for the moment. I want to live each day like it is the day you are coming.

GRACE CHECK-IN

After looking at Grace in our devotionals for the last thirteen days, you know that grace was given to us as a gift from God because of the love He has for us. It is through grace that God works effective change in our hearts and lives.

Theologians define two types of grace: common grace and special grace. Special grace is defined as having a relationship with Christ as a working of the Holy Spirit. It's what's been given to those who have been saved. Common grace is to motivate those who have been saved and not to do what's right before God. It's for all people.

List some ways in which these two types of grace show up in your life:

_____

_____

_____

_____

_____

Because of God's grace, today I can forgive myself for...

_____

_____

_____

_____

_____

_____

I am thankful for grace because...

_____

_____

_____

_____

_____

_____

Write a summary of your story of salvation.

Grace has given us a way to salvation. What led you up to the moment you gave your life to the Lord? What does God's grace mean to you in your life today?

_____

_____

_____

_____

_____

_____

_____

_____

_____

_____

_____

_____

SECTION THREE

GROWTH

You might find it helpful to look back at
this grace check-in from time to time and
document the new ways in which you're
seeing God's grace as you grow.

DAY 29

GROWTH

The seed that fell among thorns stands for those who hear, but as they go on their way they are choked by life's worries, riches, and pleasures, and they do not mature. But the seed on good soil stands for those with a noble and good heart, who hear the word, retain it, and by persevering, produce a crop.

Luke 8:14–15

Are you ready to grow in His Word, or will you stay where you are at and not go out to reach others?

Write a list of some things that you can do personally to grow with God. How can you teach others what He has done for you and what He can do for them? Will you be the one who just hears the Word, or will you live by the Word?

Prayer

God, I want to be that person who is an example to others rather than just living my life the way I want to. Help me to plant the seed and water the ones that need nourishment. Give me the words to say and the heart to speak the truth.

DAY 30

GROWTH

For this reason, since the day we heard about you, we have not stopped praying for you. We continually ask God to fill you with the knowledge of His will through all the wisdom and understanding that the Spirit gives, so that you may live a life worthy of the Lord and please him in every way: bearing fruit in every good work, growing in the knowledge of God.

Colossians 1:9–10

Growing in the Word of God is not just reading it, but speaking to Him while you do. Life can be challenging, and sometimes it is hard to pray while not knowing what to say or feeling uncomfortable because He is not physically with you. Keep in mind that His presence is always there, like one young child said to me: "Jesus is always with us, even if you can't see Him, because you can feel Him." Like a child, you might even want to pretend that He is a physical person in the room to help you focus.

Write down a couple of prayers that you would like to say to God. Maybe find a scripture that jumps out at you and turn it into a prayer. Who can you pray for today?

Prayer

God, I know you are with me every day. Help me grow in your word, and help me to understand in my heart the greatness of your love. Help me to take every opportunity to pray for others around me.

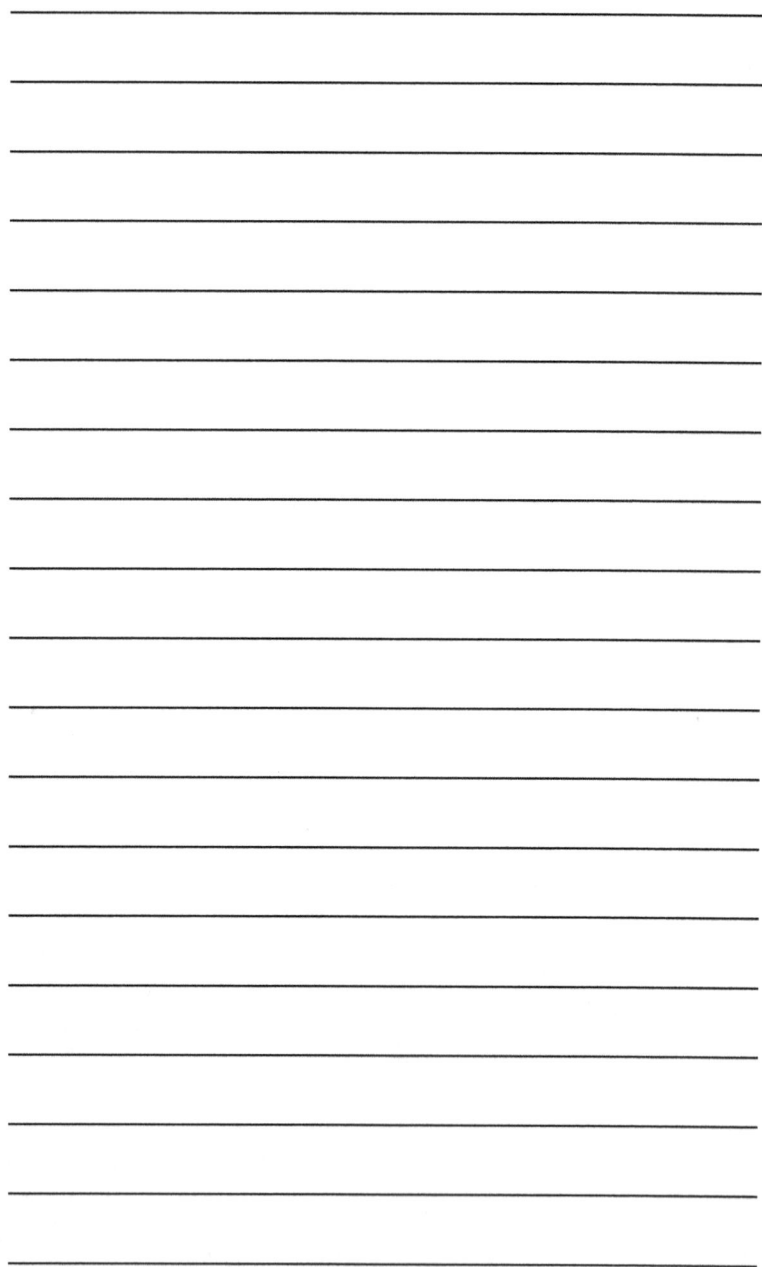

DAY 31

GROWTH

Until we all reach unity in the faith and in the knowledge of the Son of God and become mature, attaining to the whole measure of the fullness of Christ. Then we will no longer be infants, tossed back and forth by the waves, and blown here and there by every wind of teaching and by the cunning and craftiness of people in their deceitful scheming. Instead, speaking the truth in love, we will grow to become in every respect the mature body of Him who is the head, that is, Christ. From Him the whole body, joined and held together by every supporting ligament, grows and builds itself up in love, as each part does its work.

Ephesians 4:13–16

We can learn every day, no matter what the circumstances are or what life throws at us. We can learn more each day, no matter what we already know. Sometimes we feel that there isn't anything else to learn, but there is. Every day, we consistently read the Bible, pray, and ask for wisdom.

Don't take life for granted. Know that you can listen to others and ask questions along the way. We are each far from being perfect.

What are some questions you may have to ask someone to help you grow? Who can you ask the questions to? What are some scripture passages that you may not understand and need to research further?

Prayer

God, you have touched my heart in a way that I sometimes don't understand. I sometimes can't get a grip on the love you have for me, but I ask now that you will teach me and show me what I can do to learn your ways and understand your Word. I want not just to memorize scripture, but to know what it means.

GROWTH CHECK-IN

We've just spent a month in our devotionals looking at how gratitude and grace in our lives lead us to growth. Reflect on what the Lord has been teaching you in this past month.

What does growth mean to you?

- In a physical sense:

_____

_____

_____

_____

- In a spiritual sense:

_____

_____

_____

_____

- In an emotional sense:

_____

_____

_____

_____

Growth is a sense of self-improvement in your mind. What can you do going forward to grow your mind spiritually?

_____

_____

_____

_____

_____

Look up some scriptures to read that can help you grow. What scriptures did you find?

_____

_____

_____

_____

While you have been reading scripture, how has it affected your sense of well-being?

_____

_____

_____

_____

_____

_____

_____

Do you feel closer to God because of your growth?

_____

_____

_____

_____

_____

_____

_____

Who do you want to be praying for that they might grow closer to God?

_____

_____

_____

_____

_____

_____

_____

This list never needs to be complete. Commit to praying for the people God places around you to grow in their walks with Him as you grow in yours with Him!

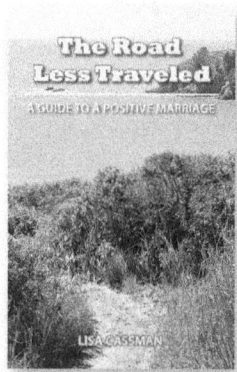

The Road Less Traveled:
A Guide to a Positive Marriage
ISBN Paperback: 978-1-61244-502-1

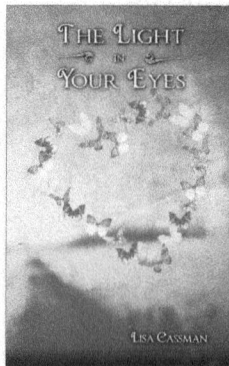

The Light in Your Eyes
ISBN Paperback: 978-1-61244-304-1

Finding the Beautiful You
ISBN Paperback: 978-1-61244-601-1

Talk Before Text:
A Prayer Journal Guide
ISBN Paperback: 978-1-61244-777-3

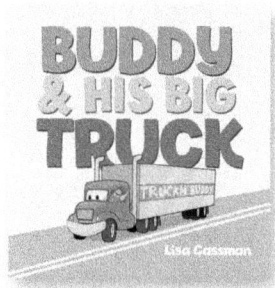

Buddy and His Big Truck
ISBN Hardcover: 978-1-63765-001-1
ISBN Paperback: 978-1-61244-991-3

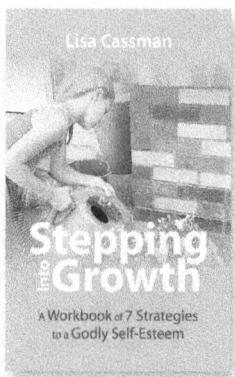

Stepping Into Growth:
A Workbook of 7 Strategies to a Godly Self-Esteem
ISBN Paperback: 978-1-63765-185-8

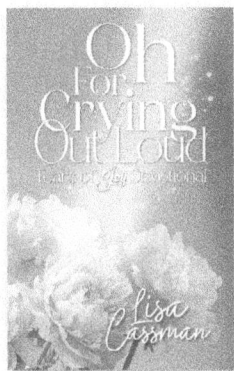

Oh For Crying Out Loud:
Tears of Joy Devotional
ISBN Paperback: 978-1-63765-586-3

AUTHOR • SPEAKER • PASTOR • LIFE COACH

Let's Connect

Get to know Lisa Cassman

Website:
www.lisacassman.com
www.findingthebeautifulyou.com

Facebook:
www.facebook.com/lcassman

www.ingramcontent.com/pod-product-compliance
Lightning Source LLC
Chambersburg PA
CBHW052005090426
42741CB00008B/1556